STERLING CHILDREN'S BOOKS
New York

An Imprint of Sterling Publishing
1166 Avenue of the Americas
New York, NY 10036

ISBN 978-1-4549-1491-4

Distributed in Canada by Sterling Publishing
C/o Canadian Manda Group, 664 Annette Street
Toronto, Ontario, Canada M6S 2C8.
Distributed in the United Kingdom by GMC Distribution Services
Castle Place, 166 High Street, Lewes, East Sussex, England BN7 1XU
Distributed in Australia by Capricorn Link (Australia) Pty. Ltd.
P.O. Box 704, Windsor, NSW 2756, Australia

For information about custom editions, special sales, and premium and corporate purchases, please contact Sterling Special Sales at 800-805-5489 or specialsales@sterlingpublishing.com.

Design by Merideth Harte

Manufactured in China
Lot #:
2 4 6 8 10 9 7 5 3 1
01/16

www.sterlingpublishing.com

AMERICAN MUSEUM ᴼᶠ NATURAL HISTORY

I Am NOT a Dinosaur!

by
WILL LACH

illustrated by
JONNY LAMBERT

with a note from
DR. MARK A. NORELL

STERLING CHILDREN'S BOOKS
New York

A Note from a Paleontologist

Many people, when they see a fossil skeleton, immediately think that it is a dinosaur. And why not? Dinosaurs run rampant through popular culture, and "museum skeleton" and "dinosaur" are almost synonymous. But they aren't. This book, based on the fossil halls at the American Museum of Natural History, tells the story of these skeletons, the majority of which are not dinosaurs. The fossil record of backboned life on our planet is a rich one, extending back over 525 million years and continuing to the present. It reveals a story of the relationships among and evolution of fishes, amphibians, mammals, lizards, crocodiles, turtles, and more. It tells us about extinction, climate change, and the fragility and resilience of species, and it documents a diversity of body forms that seems unimaginable. Museum fossil halls document this history, too. So on your next trip to a museum, remember the title *I Am NOT a Dinosaur!* Yes, dinosaurs exist, but they are only part of the story.

Dr. Mark A. Norell

Macaulay Curator of Paleontology
and Chair, Division of Paleontology
American Museum of Natural History

A long, long, long, long time ago,
strange beasts roamed Earth, both high and low,
from huge to tiny, sky to shore . . .
but—
each was *not* a dinosaur!

My formal name is *Smilodon*.
I pounce on beasts I prey upon.
Two sword-like teeth flash when I roar . . .
but—

I am **not** a dinosaur!

I am a **saber-toothed cat**.

I have no teeth, just pointy jaws—
two fierce and bony living saws.
I cut fish down right to the core ...
but—

I am **not** a dinosaur!

I am *Dunkleosteus*.

A giant sail stands on my back
to cool and scare, and—maybe—attract.
I am a scaly carnivore . . .
but—

I am *not* a dinosaur!

I am **Dimetrodon**.

I look just like an elephant
with fur and tusks so elegant.
I went extinct in days of yore ...
but—

I am **not** a dinosaur!

I am a **woolly mammoth**.

Twice as long as a great white shark,
I have 7-inch teeth to hit my mark.
I'm a very big fish at the old seashore . . .
but—

I am **not** a dinosaur!

I am *Carcharodon megalodon*.

My hunger for vegetables has no bounds.
I'm 10 feet long and 1,000 pounds!
The Americas are where I explore ...
but—

I am **not** a dinosaur!

I am a **glyptodont**.

On all four legs I humbly crawl.
But standing up, I'm 10 feet tall!
I stretch to grab leaves, like a good herbivore . . .
but—

I am **not** a dinosaur!

I am **Lestodon**.

Folks thought I was gone for millions of years.
But then, in a fisherman's net I appeared!
I lived with the dinos, and I hope to live more ...
but—

I am **not** a dinosaur!

I am **Latimeria**.

My wings are of skin—stretched finger to calf.
And my size, it can vary—from wren to giraffe.
High in the sky above *T. rex* I soar...
but—

I am **not** a dinosaur!

I am a **pterosaur**.

I may look like a dino that lives in the sea,
but that wouldn't be fair to my family tree.
I swim with flippers—oh yes, I've got four!
But—

I am **not** a dinosaur!

I am a **plesiosaur**.

"Caveman" they call me, but let's be specific:
I take care of my family, and my tools are terrific!
I'm related to you, which you cannot ignore . . .
but—

I am **not** a dinosaur!

I am a **Neanderthal**.

I'm famous, Cretaceous, a museum rock star!
(With big teeth and muscles I'll go very far.)
I'm sure that you've heard all about me before, for—

yes, I *am* a dinosaur!

I am *Tyrannosaurus rex*.

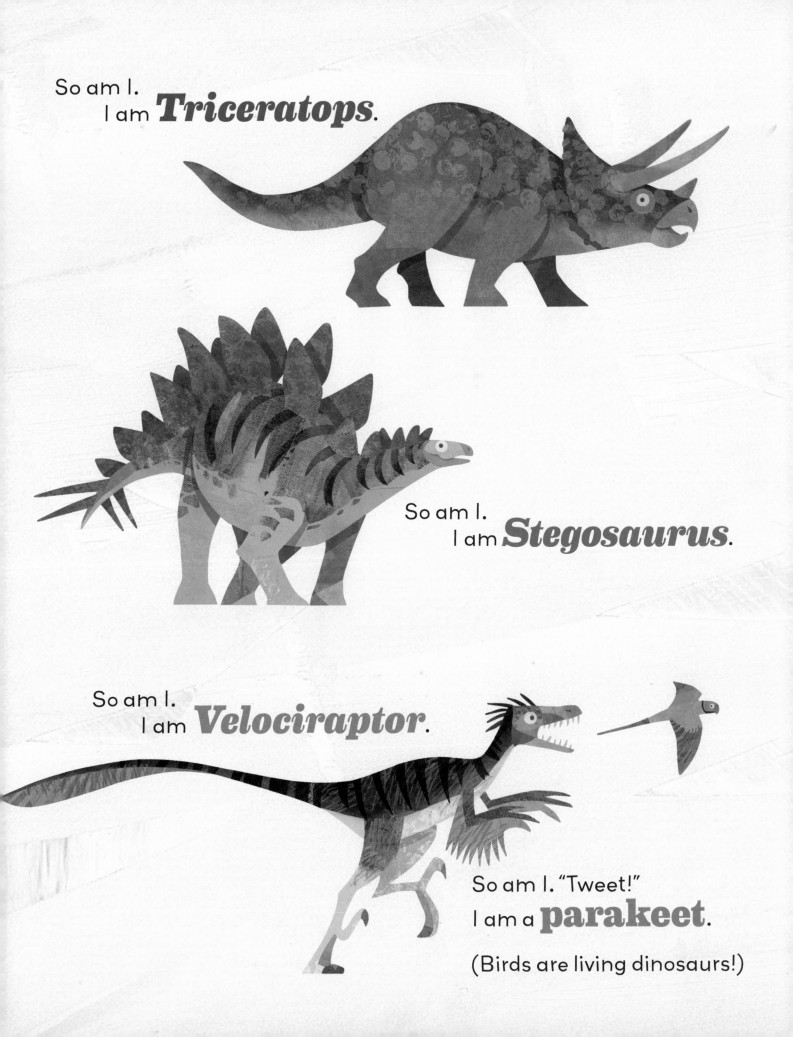

So am I.
I am **Triceratops**.

So am I.
I am **Stegosaurus**.

So am I.
I am **Velociraptor**.

So am I. "Tweet!"
I am a **parakeet**.

(Birds are living dinosaurs!)

What is a dinosaur?

Everyone knows what a dinosaur is—or *do* they?

Despite cartoonists' best efforts to convince us otherwise, you may know that dinosaurs (other than birds) never coexisted with early humans or mammoths.

You may even know that dinosaurs appeared around 235 million years ago and non-avian dinosaurs became extinct about 66 million years ago. Of course, that is a huge span of time: 170 million years. For comparison, human evolution has only been happening for the last 5 million years, with modern humans showing up about 200,000 years ago.

During this period of nearly 170 million years, old dinosaur species became extinct and new dinosaur species evolved. *T. rex* and *Triceratops*, two of the most popular species today, lived at the same time. But *Stegosaurus*, another familiar type of dinosaur, lived and went extinct nearly 80 million years before *T. rex* ever saw the light of day. (To put it another way, you and I are much closer in time to *T. rex* than *T. rex* was to *Stegosaurus*!)

Did you know that not only were there many different species of dinosaurs living at different times, but there were also creatures that lived with the dinosaurs and looked a lot like dinosaurs but weren't dinosaurs at all? Pterosaurs, for instance, the famous "flying dinosaurs," are one example of these non-dinosaurs: they were flying reptiles. *Dimetrodon*, another dinosaur-looking creature, was actually a relative of mammals that appeared 50 million years before the first dinosaurs evolved.

Dinosaurs are just one type of prehistoric creature, classified by certain physical characteristics: a hole in their hip socket, a three-toed foot, and an S-shaped neck. If we base our definition for dinosaurs on these three traits, even our long-held belief that dinosaurs went extinct isn't true. All of these characteristics you can observe in pigeons and chickens. Research shows that today's birds, from pet store parakeets to common crows, are types of dinosaurs! After this connection was made, paleontologists revised what they knew about dinosaur posture, gait, and breeding habits, among other things.

Paleontologists study creatures so old that their remains have fossilized, or turned into rock. But new research is still being done, and new discoveries are still being made at fossil sites on every continent and in museums everywhere.

About the creatures in this book

I am a **saber-toothed cat**.

The saber-toothed cat, or *Smilodon* (SMI-loh-don), did not live during the age of dinosaurs. They lived pretty recently—up until about 10,000 years ago—along with other Ice Age creatures, such as mammoths, glyptodonts, and giant ground sloths.

I am *Dunkleosteus*.

The razor-sharp edges of the jawbones of the 20-foot-long *Dunkleosteus* (DUN-kel-OS-tee-us) were great cutters. These jaw blades were like self-sharpening scissors. They continued to grow in length until worn down by use.

I am *Dimetrodon*.

Although it looks like a reptile, the *Dimetrodon* (dye-MEH-tro-don) was an early relative of mammals, and it lived 50 million years before dinosaurs evolved. The large "sail" on its back may have been used for cooling off, scaring other animals, or attracting mates.

I am a **woolly mammoth**.

Woolly mammoths stood 9 to 11 feet tall, and weighed 4 to 6 tons. To protect their skin from freezing weather, they had a layer of fat and thick layers of hair, much like today's musk oxen. (The fossil shown above in the Museum's gallery is actually that of the closely related American mammoth, which was not hairy.)

I am *Carcharodon megalodon*.

Sharks have been around for over 400 million years! The most famous extinct shark, *Carcharodon megalodon* (kar-KAR-o-don MEG-a-LO-don), lived 10 million years ago and was probably two to three times as large as today's great white sharks.

I am a **glyptodont**.

The enormous, plant-eating glyptodont (GLIP-toe-donnt) shuffled across North and South America for millions of years. Early relatives of armadillos, glyptodonts could be as large as cars: up to 10 feet long!

About the creatures in this book

I am *Lestodon*.

Giant ground sloths lived in the Americas and died out 5,000 years ago. This sloth, or *Lestodon* (LES-toe-don), is considered an armored mammal because it had bony plates in its skin for extra protection.

I am *Latimeria*.

Coelacanths (SEEL-uh-canths) were thought to have gone extinct about 70 million years ago. In 1938, a fisherman caught a living one, now known as *Latimeria chalumnae* (LAD-uh-MAIR-ee-uh kuh-LUM-nee), off the coast of South Africa. This is one of only two known living species of coelacanths.

I am a **pterosaur**.

Pterosaurs (TEH-rah-soars) are flying reptiles, close cousins of dinosaurs but on a separate branch of the reptile family tree. The smallest had a 6-inch wingspan, and the largest stood about 12 feet tall! Their wings of skin stretched from their long "ring fingers" to below their "knees."

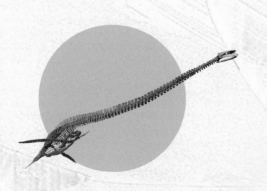

I am a **plesiosaur**.

While dinosaurs were the top predators on land, three groups of large prehistoric reptiles—plesiosaurs (PLES-ee-oh-soars), mosasaurs (MOS-a-soars), and ichthyosaurs (ICK-thee-oh-soars)—dominated the food chain in the oceans.

I am a **Neanderthal**.

First appearing between 250,000 and 28,000 years ago, Neanderthals (nee-ANN-der-talls) had brains as large as ours. They were outstanding toolmakers who lived in social groups and took care of one another.

About the creatures in this book

I am *Tyrannosaurus rex*.

Tyrannosaurus rex (tih-RAN-o-SAW-rus reks) had great power and was one of the fiercest dinosaurs that ever existed. It had a 4-foot jaw, 6-inch teeth, and massive thigh bones.

I am *Triceratops*.

Triceratops (tri-SER-ah-tops) had three horns on its face and a large bony "frill" projecting from its skull. Its horns were covered in material similar to human fingernails.

I am *Stegosaurus*.

At one time, some scientists thought *Stegosaurus* (STEG-o-SAW-rus) had a second brain because the one in its head seemed so small. *Stegosaurus*'s seventeen bony plates, like *Dimetrodon*'s "sail," were likely used for scaring off predators or attracting mates.

I am *Velociraptor*.

Although only the size of a coyote, *Velociraptor* (ve-LOS-ih-RAP-tor) was a fierce predator. It had sharp teeth, but its deadliest weapon was a huge talon on each of its feet, with which it could rip into flesh.

I am a **parakeet**.

Scientists consider birds to be living dinosaurs. The traits that we see in birds—their anatomy, the presence of feathers, and behaviors like nesting—were common in some dinosaurs.

Late Devonian period

Permian period

Late Jurassic period

Late Cretaceous period

DUNKLEOSTEUS

Dunkleosteus species lived about 360 million years ago, during the Late Devonian period.

DIMETRODON

Dimetrodon limbatus lived about 280 million years ago, in the Permian period.

PLESIOSAUR

Cryptoclidus oxoniensis lived about 150 million years ago, during the Late Jurassic period.

STEGOSAURUS

Stegosaurus stenops lived about 140 million years ago, during the Late Jurassic period.

VELOCIRAPTOR

Velociraptor mongoliensis lived about 72 million years ago, during the Late Cretaceous period.

PTEROSAUR

Pterosaurs lived from about 228 to 66 million years ago, during the Late Cretaceous period.

T. REX

Tyrannosaurus rex lived about 66 million years ago, during the Late Cretaceous period.

TRICERATOPS

Triceratops horridus lived about 66 million years ago, during the Late Cretaceous period.

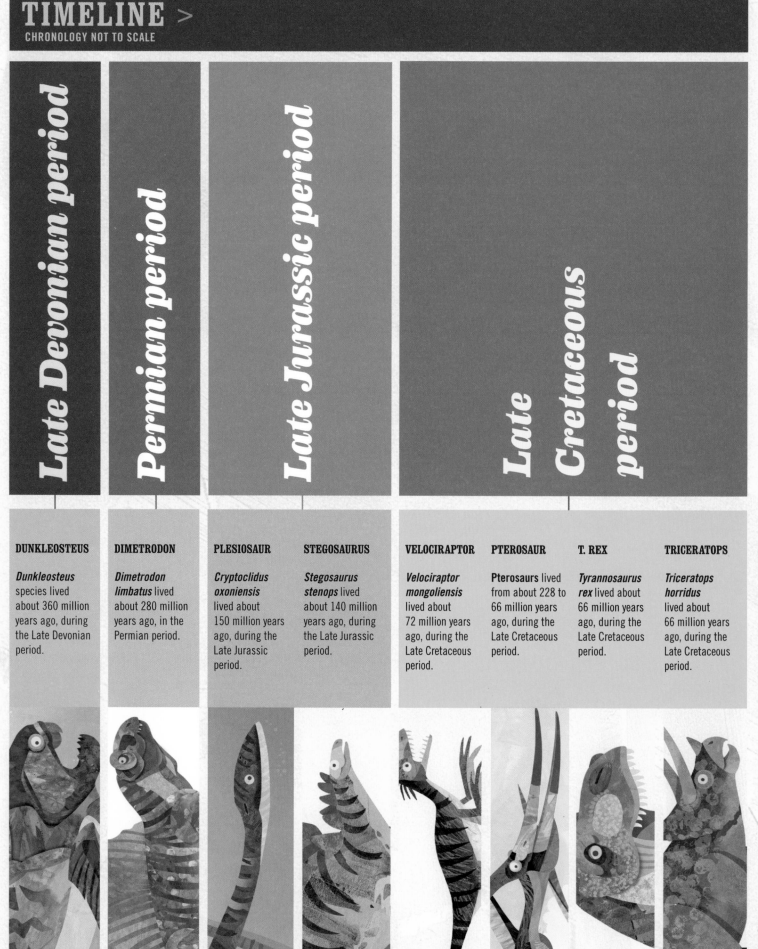

Late Miocene epoch

Pleistocene epoch

Present day

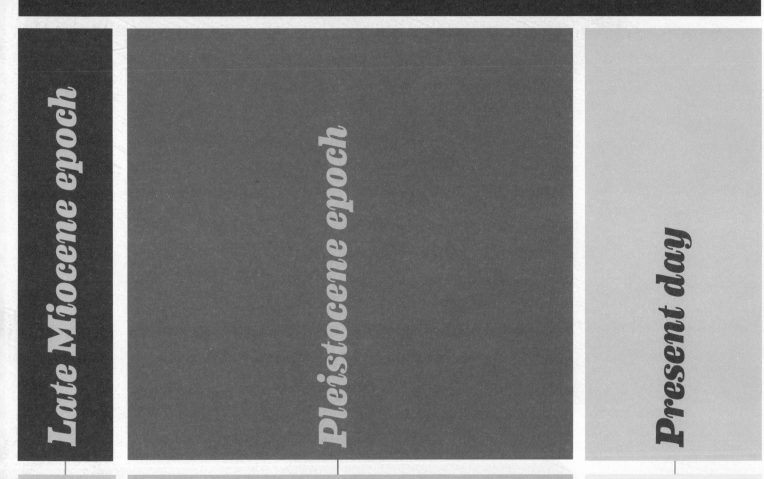

CARCHARODON MEGALODON

Carcharodon megalodon lived about 10 million years ago, during the late Miocene epoch.

NEANDERTHAL

Homo neanderthalensis lived 250,000 to 28,000 years ago, in the Pleistocene epoch.

LESTODON

Lestodon armatus lived about 30,000 years ago, in the Pleistocene epoch.

GLYPTODONT

Panochthus frenzelianus lived about 30,000 years ago, in the Pleistocene epoch.

SABER-TOOTHED CAT

Smilodon floridanus lived about 25,000 years ago, in the Pleistocene epoch.

WOOLLY MAMMOTH

Mammuthus primigenius lived about 10,000 years ago, in the Pleistocene epoch.

LATIMERIA

Latimeria chalumnae are alive today.

PARAKEET

Birds are living dinosaurs.

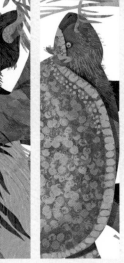